PRESENTED
TO

....

THE CROSS

©1998, 2002 by Max Lucado
published by Multnomah Publishers, Inc.
P.O. Box 1720, Sisters, Oregon 97759

ISBN 1-57673-920-1

Artwork and design by Koechel Peterson & Associates, Minneapolis, Minnesota

Selections from Max Lucado's writings are taken from:
And the Angels Were Silent © 1992 by Max Lucado
Multnomah Publishers, Inc. All rights reserved.
God Came Near © 1987 by Max Lucado
Multnomah Publishers, Inc. All rights reserved.
No Wonder They Call Him the Savior © 1986 by Max Lucado
Multnomah Publishers, Inc. All rights reserved.
Six Hours One Friday © 1989 by Max Lucado
Multnomah Publishers, Inc. All rights reserved.

The Holy Bible, New International Version
1973, 1984 by International Bible Society,
used by permission of Zondervan Publishing House

The Holy Bible, New King James Version (NKJV)
1984 by Thomas Nelson, Inc.

The Holy Bible, King James Version (KJV)

The Holy Bible, New Century Version (NCV)
©1987, 1988, 1991 by Word Publishing. Used by permission.

Printed in China

Library of Congress Cataloging-in-Publication Data:
The Cross / by Max Lucado.
p. cm
ISBN 1-57673-093-X (alk. paper)
ISBN 1-57673-920-1
1.   Crosses–Pictorial works. 2. Jesus Christ–Crucifixion–
      Quotations, maxims, etc. I. Multnomah Publishers.
      BV160.C76 1997
      246'.558–dc21

                                                    96–40126
                                                      CIP

02 03 04 05 06 07 08—10 9 8 7 6 5 4

www.multnomahgifts.com

MAX LUCADO

THE CROSS

MULTNOMAH GIFTS™

Multnomah®Publishers Sisters, Oregon

IT RESTS ON THE

TIME LINE OF HISTORY

LIKE A COMPELLING

DIAMOND.

Its tragedy summons all sufferers. Its absurdity attracts all cynics. Its hope lures all searchers. History has idolized and despised it, gold-plated and burned it, worn and trashed it. History has done everything but ignore it. How could you? How could you ignore such a piece of lumber? Suspended on its beams is the greatest claim in history. A crucified carpenter claiming to be God on earth. Divine. Eternal. The death-slayer. Never has timber been regarded so sacred. No wonder the apostle Paul called the cross event the core of the gospel (1 CORINTHIANS 13:3–5). Its bottom line is sobering: if the account is true, it is history's hinge. Period. If not, the cross is history's hoax. As you ponder Christ on the cross, what are your thoughts? Perhaps it's been a while since you looked at the cross. Perhaps you never have. May I urge you to do so? Allow the turning of these pages to trigger a turning of your heart until you stand face to feet with the one who claimed to come to save your soul.

HEAVEN'S DREAM

The dawn of heaven's dream. God on a cross. Humanity at its worst. Divinity at its best.... God isn't stumped by an evil world. He doesn't gasp in amazement at the dearth of our faith or the depth of our failures. He knows the condition of the world...and loves it just the same. For just when we find a place where God would never be (like on a cross), we look again and there he is, in the flesh.

God on a cross? The creator of the universe sacrificing himself for his creation? How could this be? Who was this Jesus?

He was—and is—a God with tears. A creator with a heart. Bloodstained royalty. A God who became earth's mockery to save his children.

How absurd to think that such nobility would go to such poverty to share such a treasure with such thankless souls. How incredible to know that God himself died on a cross for his children.

But he did.

Incredible.

Yes, incredibly, he did.

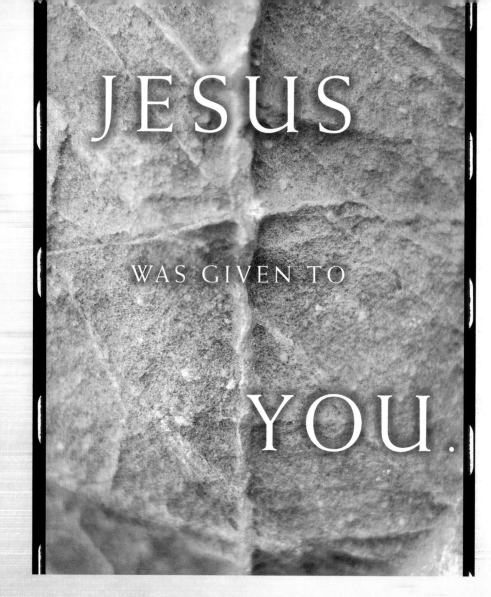

JESUS

WAS GIVEN TO

YOU.

And with the help of those who don't know the law, you put him to death by nailing him to a cross. But this was God's plan, which he had made long ago; he knew this would happen. God raised Jesus from the dead and set him free from the pain of death, because death could not hold him (ACTS 2:23–24). The cross was no accident.

Jesus' death was not the result of a panicking cosmological engineer. The cross was not a tragic surprise. Calvary was not a knee-jerk response to a world plummeting toward destruction. It was not a patch-up job or a stopgap measure. The death of the Son of God was anything but an unexpected peril.

No, it was part of an incredible plan. A calculated choice. "It was the Lord's will to crush him" (ISAIAH 53:10).

The moment the forbidden fruit touched the lips of Eve, the shadow of a cross appeared on the horizon. And between that moment and the moment the man with the mallet placed the spike against the wrist of God, a master plan was fulfilled.

What does that mean? It means Jesus planned his own sacrifice.
It means Jesus intentionally planted the tree from which his cross would
be carved. It means he willingly placed the iron ore in the heart of the
earth from which the nails would be cast.

It means he voluntarily placed his Judas in the womb of a woman.

It means Christ was the one who set in motion the political machinery
that would send Pilate to Jerusalem.

And it also means he didn't have to do it—but he did. It was no accident—
would that it had been! Even the cruelest of criminals is spared
the agony of having his death sentence read to him before his life
even begins.

But Jesus was born crucified. Whenever he became conscious
of who he was, he also became conscious of what he had to do.
The cross-shaped shadow could always be seen. And the screams
of hell's imprisoned could always be heard.

This explains the glint of determination on his face as he turned to go
to Jerusalem for the last time. He was on his death march (LUKE 9:51).

"LOOK, THE

LAMB OF GOD,

WHO TAKES AWAY THE SIN

OF THE WORLD!"

JOHN 1:29

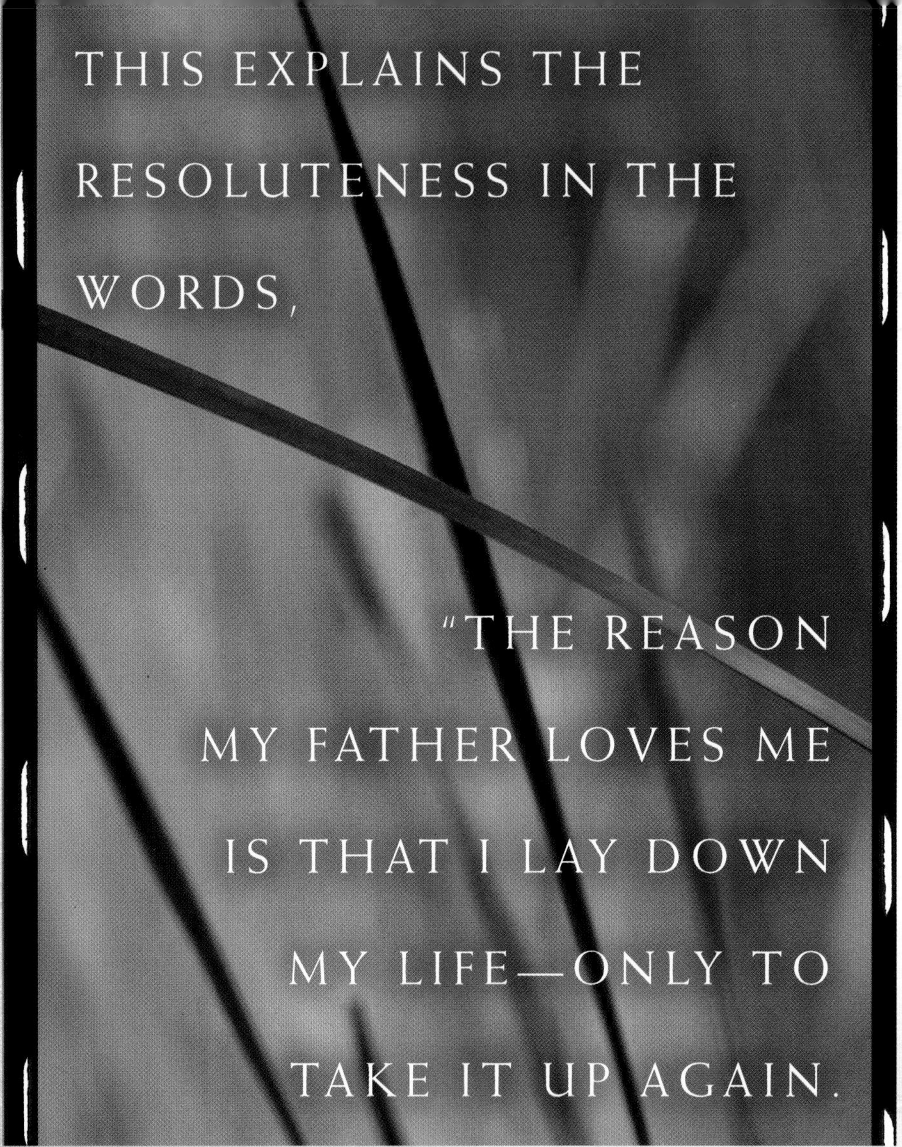

THIS EXPLAINS THE
RESOLUTENESS IN THE
WORDS,

"THE REASON
MY FATHER LOVES ME
IS THAT I LAY DOWN
MY LIFE—ONLY TO
TAKE IT UP AGAIN.

"No one takes it from me, but I lay it down of my own accord" (JOHN 10:17–18).

It explains the enigmatic question, "Does this offend you? What if you see the Son of Man ascend to where he was before!" (JOHN 6:61–62).

The cross explains…

Why he told the Pharisees that the "goal" of his life would be fulfilled only on the third day after his death (LUKE 13:32).

The mysterious appearance of Moses and Elijah on the Mount of Transfiguration to discuss his "departure" (LUKE 9:30–31). They'd come to offer one last word of encouragement.

Why John the Baptist introduced Jesus to the crowds as the "Lamb of God, who takes away the sin of the world!" (JOHN 1:29).

Maybe it's why he tore the grass out by the roots in Gethsemane. He knew the hell he'd endure for saying, "Thy will be done."

Maybe the cross was why he so loved children. They represented the very thing he would have to give: life.

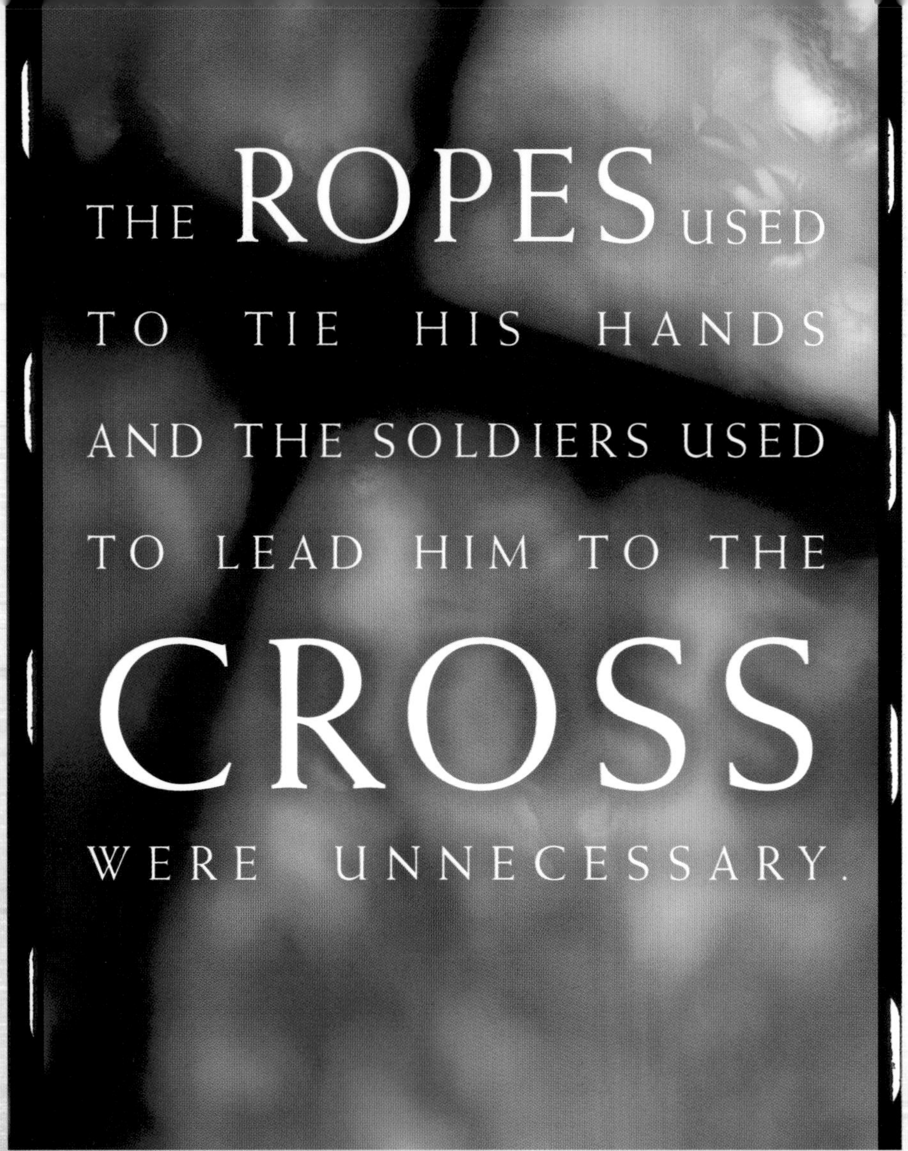

THE ROPES USED
TO TIE HIS HANDS
AND THE SOLDIERS USED
TO LEAD HIM TO THE
CROSS
WERE UNNECESSARY.

They were incidental. Had they not been there, had there been no trial, no Pilate, and no crowd, the very same crucifixion would have occurred. Had Jesus been forced to nail himself to the cross, he would have done it. For it was not the soldiers who killed him, nor the screams of the mob: It was his devotion to us.

So call it what you wish: An act of grace. A plan of redemption. A martyr's sacrifice. But whatever you call it, don't call it an accident. It was anything but that.

Jesus didn't take a wrong turn that led him to the cross. He marked the path and marched purposely to Calvary.

Forget any suggestion that Jesus was trapped. Erase any theory that Jesus made a miscalculation. Ignore any speculation that the cross was a last-ditch attempt to salvage a dying mission.

Jesus went to the cross on purpose. No surprise. No hesitation. No faltering.

You can tell a lot about a person by the way he dies. And the way Jesus marched to his death leaves no doubt: He had come to earth for this moment. Read the words of Peter.

"Jesus was given to you, and with the help of those who don't know the law, you put him to death by nailing him to a cross. But this was God's plan which he had made long ago; he knew all this would happen" (ACTS 2:23–24, NCV).

The journey to the cross didn't begin in Galilee. It didn't begin in Nazareth. It did not even begin in Bethlehem.

The journey to the cross began long before. As the echo of the crunching of the fruit was still sounding in the garden, Jesus was leaving for Calvary.

God on a cross. The ultimate act of creative compassion. The Creator being sacrificed for the creation. God convincing man once and for all that he would give anything, pay any price to save his children.

He could have given up. He could have turned his back. He could have walked away from the wretched mess the world became, but he didn't.

God didn't give up.

WHEN PEOPLE FROM HIS

OWN HOMETOWN TRIED TO

PUSH HIM OVER A CLIFF,

HE DIDN'T

GIVE UP.

When his brothers ridiculed him, he didn't give up.

When he was accused of blaspheming God by people who didn't fear God, he didn't give up.

When Peter worshiped him at the supper and cursed him at the fire, he didn't give up.

When people spat in his face, he didn't spit back. When the bystanders slapped him, he didn't slap them. When a whip ripped his sides, he didn't turn and command the awaiting angels to stuff that whip down that soldier's throat.

And when human hands fastened the divine hands to a cross with spikes, it was not the soldiers who held the hands of Jesus steady. It was God who held them steady. Those same hands that formed the oceans and built the mountains. Those same hands that designed the dawn and crafted each cloud. Those same hands that blueprinted one incredible plan for you and me. Take a stroll out to the hill. Out to Calvary. Out to the cross where, with holy blood, the hand that placed you on the planet wrote the promise: "God would give up his only Son before he'd give up on you."

God is on a cross. The creator of the universe is being executed.

Spit and blood are caked to his cheeks, and his lips are cracked and swollen. Thorns rip his scalp. His lungs scream with pain. His legs knot with cramps. Taut nerves threaten to snap as pain twangs her morbid melody. Yet death is not ready. And there is no one to save him, for he is sacrificing himself.

Far worse than the breaking of his body is the shredding of his heart.

His own countrymen clamored for his death.

His own disciple planted the kiss of betrayal.

His own friends ran for cover.

And now his own father is beginning to turn his back on him, leaving him alone....

SACRED SYMBOL

FINALLY

THE HOUR

CAME.

The Son went for one last visit with his Father. He met him in a garden of gnarled trees and stony soil.

"Does it have to be this way?" asked the Son.

"It does," whispered the Father.

"Is there no one else who can do it?"

The Father swallowed. "None but you." He looked at his Son, the Prince of Light. "The darkness will be great." He passed his hand over the spotless face of his Son. "The pain will be awful." Then he paused and looked at his darkened dominion. When he looked up, his eyes were moist. "But there is no other way."

The Son looked into the stars as he heard the answer. "Then let it be done."

Slowly the words that would kill the Son began to come from the lips of the Father.

"Hour of death, moment of sacrifice, it is your moment. Rehearsed a million times on false altars with false lambs; the moment of truth has come.

"Soldiers, you think you lead him? Ropes, you think you bind him?

"Men, you think you sentence him? He heeds not your commands. He winces not at your lashes. It is my voice he obeys. It is my condemnation he dreads. And it is your souls he saves.

"Oh, my Son, my Child. Look up into the heavens and see my face before I turn it. Hear my voice before I silence it. Would that I could save you and them. But they don't see and they don't hear.

"The living must die so that the dying can live. The time has come to kill the Lamb.

"Here is the cup, my Son. The cup of sorrows. The cup of sin.

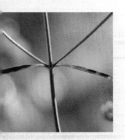

"Slam, mallet! Be true to your task. Let your ring be heard throughout the heavens.

"Lift him, soldiers. Lift him high to his throne of mercy. Lift him up to his perch of death. Lift him above the people that curse his name.

"Now plunge the tree into the earth. Plunge it deep into the heart of humanity. Deep into the strata of time past. Deep into the seeds of time future.

"Is there no angel to save my Isaac? Is there no hand to redeem the Redeemer?

"Here is the cup, my Son. Drink it alone."

God must have wept as he performed his task. Every lie, every lure, every act done in shadows was in that cup. Slowly, hideously they were absorbed into the body of the Son. The final act of incarnation. The spotless Lamb was blemished.

The King turns away from his Prince. The undiluted wrath of a sin-hating Father falls upon his sin-filled Son. The fire envelops him. The shadows hide him. The Son looks for his Father, but the Father cannot be seen.

"My God, my God…why?"

It was the most gut-wrenching cry of loneliness in history, and it came not from a prisoner or a widow or a patient. It came from a hill, from a cross, from a Messiah.

"My God, my God," he screamed, "why did you abandon me!"

Never have words carried such hurt. Never has one being been so lonely.

The despair is darker than the sky. The two who have been one are now two. Jesus, who had been with God for eternity, is now alone. The Christ, who was an expression of God, is abandoned. The Trinity is dismantled. The Godhead is disjointed. The unity is dissolved.

It is more than Jesus can take. He withstood the beatings and remained strong at the mock trials. He watched in silence as those he loved ran away. He did not retaliate when the insults were hurled nor did he scream when the nails pierced his wrists.

But when God turned his head, that was more than he could handle.

"My God!" The wail rises from parched lips. The holy heart is broken.

The sinbearer screams as he wanders in the eternal wasteland. Out of the silent sky come the words screamed by all who walk in the desert of loneliness. "Why? Why did you abandon me?"

I can't understand it. I honestly cannot. Why did Jesus do it? Oh, I know, I know. I have heard the official answers. "To gratify the old law." "To fulfill prophecy." And these answers are right. They are. But there is something more here. Something very compassionate. Something yearning. Something personal.

What is it?

Could it be that his heart was broken for all the people who cast despairing eyes toward the dark heavens and cry the same "Why"?

Could it be that his heart was broken for the hurting? Could his desire to take on their pain have propelled him to the cross? If he could, wouldn't he have run to the cross on behalf of all the pain in the world?

I imagine him bending close to those who hurt. I imagine him listening. I picture his eyes misting and a pierced hand brushing away a tear. And although he may offer no answer, although he may solve no dilemma, although the question may freeze painfully in midair, he who also was once alone, understands.

Are any words in history more splendid? Three words, at once shattering and victorious.

"It is finished."

Stop and listen a moment. Let the words wind through your heart. Imagine the cry from the cross. The sky is dark. The other two victims are moaning. Jeering mouths of the crowd are silent. Perhaps there is thunder. Perhaps there is weeping. Perhaps there is silence. Then Jesus draws in a deep breath, pushes his feet down on that Roman nail, and cries, "It is finished."

WHAT WAS
FINISHED?

The history-long plan of redeeming man was finished. The message of God to man was finished. The works done by Jesus as a man on earth were finished. The task of selecting and training ambassadors was finished. The job was finished. The song had been sung. The blood had been poured. The sacrifice had been made. The sting of death had been removed. It was over.

A cry of defeat? Hardly. Had his hands not been fastened down I dare say that a triumphant fist would have punched the dark sky. No, this is no cry of despair. It is a cry of completion. A cry of relief. A roar of fulfillment. A shout of victory.

SHADOW OF THE CROSS

IN THE SHADOW OF THE CROSS

Calvary is a hybrid of God's lofty

status and his deep devotion.

The thunderclap that echoed when

God's sovereignty collided with his love.

The marriage of heaven's kingship

and heaven's compassion,

a vertical beam of holiness

intersecting with the horizontal bar of love.

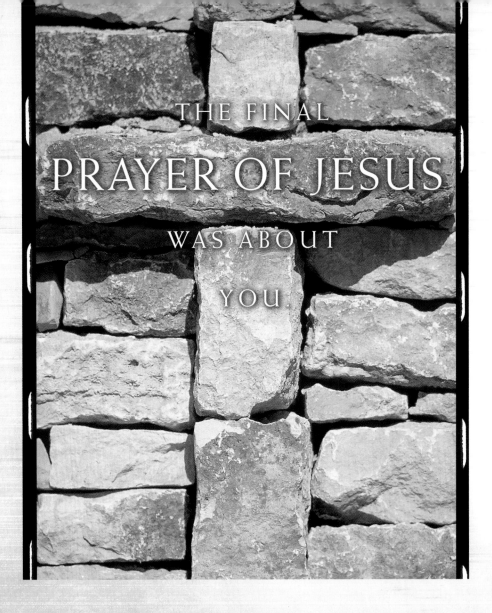

THE FINAL

PRAYER OF JESUS

WAS ABOUT

YOU

His final pain was for you. His final passion was you. Before he went to the cross, Jesus went to the Garden. And when he spoke with his Father, you were in his prayers. As Jesus looked into heaven, you were in his vision. As Jesus dreamed of the day when we will be where he is, he saw you there....

Never had he felt so alone. What had to be done, only he could do. An angel couldn't do it. No angel has the power to break open hell's gates. A man couldn't do it. No man has the purity to destroy sin's claim. No force on earth can face the force of evil and win—except God.

And God couldn't turn his back on you. He couldn't because he saw you, and one look at you was all it took to convince him. Right there in the middle of a world that isn't fair. He saw you cast into a river of life you did not request. He saw you betrayed by those you love. He saw you with a body that gets sick and a heart that grows weak.

He saw you in your own garden of gnarled trees and sleeping friends. He saw you staring into the pit of your own failures and the mouth of your own grave.

He saw you in your Garden of Gethsemane—and he didn't want you to be alone.

He wanted you to know that he has been there, too. He knows what it's like to be plotted against. He knows what it's like to be confused. He knows what it's like to be torn between two desires. He knows what it's like to smell the stench of Satan. And, perhaps most of all, he knows what it's like to beg God to change his mind and to hear God say so gently, but firmly, "No."

For that is what God said to Jesus. And Jesus accepted the answer. At some moment during that midnight hour an angel of mercy came over the weary body of the man in the Garden. Jesus stood, the anguish gone from his eyes. His heart will fight no more.

The battle has been won. The sign of conquest? Jesus at peace in the olive trees.

On the eve of the cross, Jesus made his decision. He would rather go to hell for you than go to heaven without you.

And going to the cross was the cost of his decision. Man by himself could not, cannot deal with his own guilt. He must have help from the outside.

In order to forgive himself, he must have forgiveness from the one he has offended. Yet man is unworthy to ask God for forgiveness.

That, then, is the whole reason for the cross.

The cross did what sacrificed lambs could not do. It erased our sins for eternity. The cross did what man could not do. It granted us the right to talk with, love, and even live with God.

You can't do that by yourself. No matter how many worship services you attend or good deeds you do, your goodness is insufficient. You cannot be good enough to deserve forgiveness. No one bats a thousand. No one bowls three hundred. No one. Not you, not me, nor anyone.

That's why we have guilt in the world.

That's why we need a savior.

That's why there was a cross.

You can't forgive me for my sins nor can I forgive you for yours. Two kids in a mud puddle can't clean each other. They need someone clean. Someone spotless. We need someone clean, too.

That's why we need a savior. That's why there was a cross.

"FATHER,

FORGIVE THEM;

FOR THEY KNOW NOT WHAT THEY DO."

LUKE 23:34, KJV

There was a cross so that, regardless of our behavior, despite our sins, no matter how bad we are, we could have the shining hope of an eternal residence with the lamb who took it all away.

That's why there was a cross. Have you stood near the cross? Have you made a choice for the Savior?

There's something about the cross...it seems to demand a choice. You either step toward it or away from it. It's the watershed. It's the Continental Divide. You are either on one side or the other. A choice is demanded. We can do what we want with the cross. We can examine its history. We can study its theology. We can reflect upon its prophecies. Yet the one thing we can't do is walk away, neutral. No fence-sitting is permitted. The cross, in its absurd splendor, doesn't allow that.

And so we conclude our journey to the cross. We've reflected on the heavenly plan that set the cross in place. We've anguished at the pain. And now we marvel at the promise. For that's the essence of the cross. Through all the pain, the cross is still our promise, the eternal lifeline for our spirits.

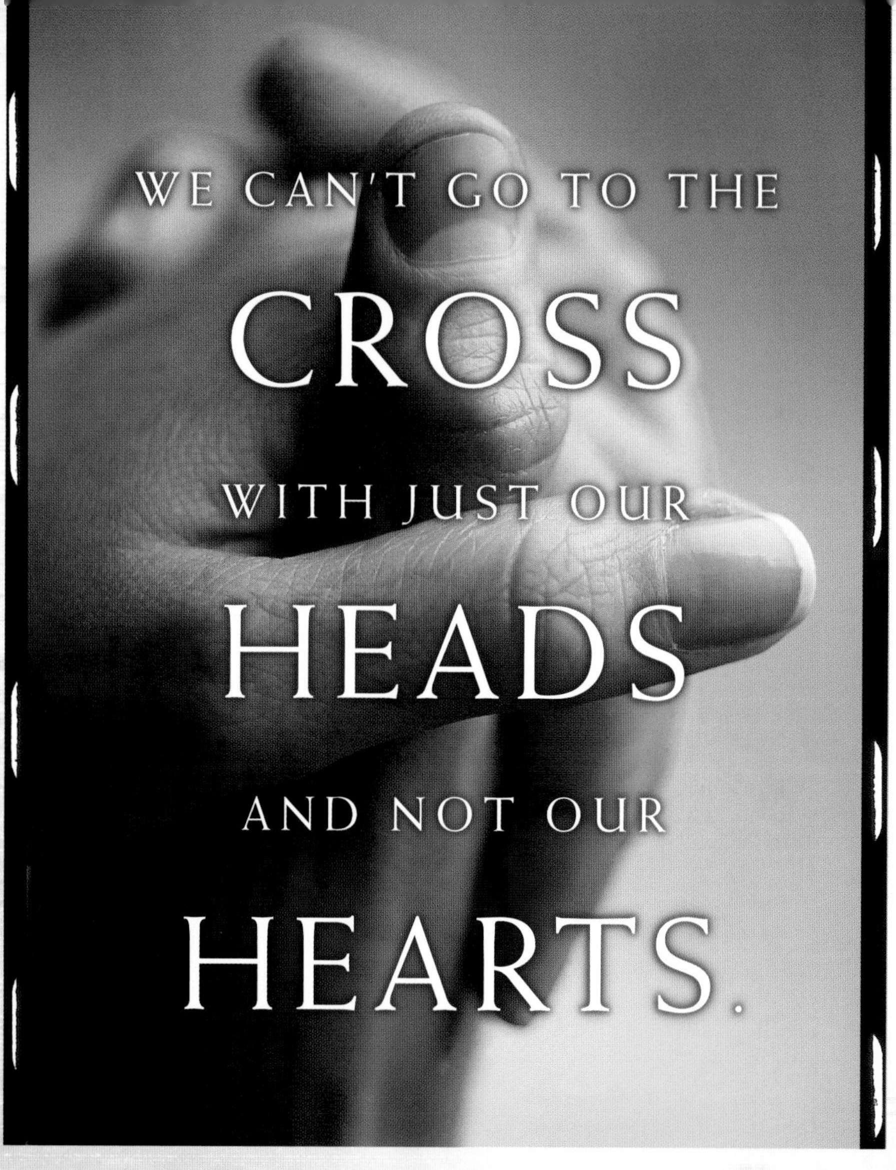

WE CAN'T GO TO THE

CROSS

WITH JUST OUR

HEADS

AND NOT OUR

HEARTS.

It doesn't work that way. Calvary is not a mental trip. It's not an intellectual exercise. It's not a divine calculation or a cold theological principle.

It's a heart-splitting hour of emotion.

Don't walk away from it dry-eyed and unstirred. Don't just straighten your tie and clear your throat. Don't allow yourself to descend Calvary cool and collected.

Please…pause. Look again.

Those are nails in those hands.

That's God on that cross.

It's us who put him there.

Peter knew it. John knew it. Mary knew it.

They knew a great price was being paid. They knew who really pierced his side. They also somehow knew that history was being remade.

That's why they wept.

They saw the Savior.

God, may we never be so educated, may we never be so mature, may we never be so religious that we can see your passion without tears.

The tragedies of September 11, 2001, were documented by dozens of gripping photos. None grabbed my heart like the picture of the cross-shaped I-beams. The image of the cross over the rubble is a symbol for our lives.

Has God not done the same for us? Has He not suspended His cross over the wreckage of our mistakes? He places His sacrifice over our divorces, our debts, our misdeeds, our missteps. He takes our ruins and renders them His victories.

May God find in your heart what the workers found in the disaster of the World Trade Center. May He find deep within you a cross…a cross forged by the heat of life's hurts. And may that cross be suspended for all to see.

Father,

May our souls be branded by your cross.

May the memory of your sacrifice ignite us.

May the song of our hearts and the expression

of our lives be, "Jesus. Jesus. Jesus!"

Amen.

A NOTE FROM THE AUTHOR

May I express thanks to some friends who made this project possible?
Being that this book is a compilation of my previous writings, I had the
privilege of sitting back and watching others do the hard part. This project
was birthed in the creative halls of Multnomah Publishers.
A special thanks to you, Don Jacobson, for your friendship and
vision. And I send equal appreciation to your talented team. Karen
Hill, my assistant, added her valuable touch by assembling the
quotes and linking thoughts. Thank you, Karen, for your dedicated
service. Steve Green, my dear friend and representative, made this and a
hundred other works smoother by doing stuff well that I do so poorly. Thanks,
pal. Most of all, I thank the reader of this book. My prayer for you is simple.
May the end result of your reading not be merely: What beautiful images or
what a good book. But may your thoughts be:What a Savior!

Such were the thoughts of another who stood where you stand. Like
you, he came to witness the cross event. From where he came, we are not
told. Where he went, we never learn. What we do know is what he said.
After beholding Christ and his death on the cross, the Centurion was led to
conclude, "Surely this man must be the Son of God." Stand on the hill of
hope and see if you don't agree.